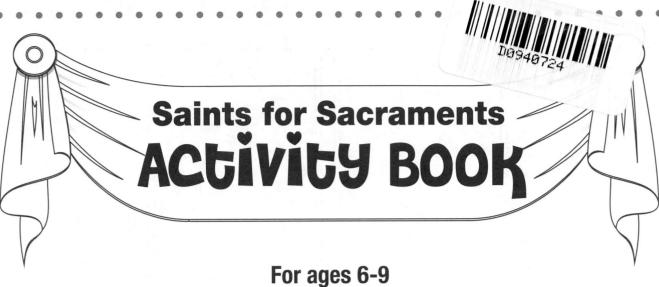

Saints for Sacraments
ACTIVITY BOOK

For ages 6-9

Reproducible pages are perforated for easy copying

SAINTS · FOR · SACRAMENTS

Saints AND me!

Liguori

John the Baptist

Padre Pio

Teresa of Ávila

Philip Neri

Louis + Zélie Martin

John Vianney

Maximilian Kolbe

Imprimi Potest:
Stephen T. Rehrauer, CSsR, Provincial
Denver Province, the Redemptorists

Published by Liguori Publications
Liguori, Missouri 63057

To order, visit Liguori.org or call 800-325-9521

ISBN 978-0-7648-2801-0

Liguori Publications, a nonprofit corporation, is an apostolate of the Redemptorists.
To learn more about the Redemptorists, visit Redemptorists.com.

Printed in the United States of America
23 22 21 20 19 / 5 4 3 2 1
First Edition

How to Use This Book

This book contains reproducible coloring and activity pages to reinforce the stories of the eight saints in the seven-book *Saints and Me! Saints for Sacraments* set: John the Baptist (baptism), Padre Pio (reconciliation), Teresa of Ávila (Eucharist), Philip Neri (confirmation), Louis and Zélie Martin (matrimony), John Vianney (holy orders), and Maximilian Kolbe (anointing of the sick). The pages are perforated, making it easy for purchasers to create copies for personal use at home or in the classroom. Each page serves as a saint- and story-based review. Several can be gathered into a single lesson or unit evaluation. Altogether, this book creates hours of enrichment and entertainment for children. After an activity is done, ask the kids to color the page, too! A key for some of the answers is in the back of this book.

Help Jesus find John the Baptist on the Jordan River so he can be baptized.

WHAT WOULD JESUS EAT?

Circle 6 foods that people might eat or drink in the Holy Land during Bible times.

dates

fish

soda pop

bread

pizza

figs

wine

honey

hamburger

SPOT THE
DIFFERENCES
DIFFERENCES

Can you circle 6 differences between the two pictures of Jesus being baptized by John the Baptist?

Answers on page 78

JOHN'S STORY

Fill in the blanks in this short story about John the Baptist. Use the words from the word bank.

When John grew up, he went to the _____ to pray and listen to God's voice. Then he traveled to the _____ _____ to baptize and preach to his _____. "Jesus the_____ is coming soon! Get ready!" he said. When Jesus came, John _____ him. The _____ _____ came down as a _____. And a voice came from heaven, "You are my ____. I am pleased with you."

WORD BANK

BAPTIZED   HOLY SPIRIT
DESERT   JORDAN RIVER
DISCIPLES   MESSIAH
DOVE   SON

Answers on page 78

PRAYER TO JOHN THE BAPTIST

Saint John
the Baptist,
You told people to
repent. You changed
people's hearts and
lives so they could
follow Jesus.
Open my heart
to do God's work
so I may grow
in holiness and love.
Amen.

dot-to-dot

Connect the dots to complete the scene on the Jordan River.

26
25
24
22 21
23   20
27   19
28   18 17
29   15 16
13 14
12
1   11
2   10
3   9
4   8
5 6 7

WORD JUMBLE

These words from the John the Baptist book are all mixed up!
Can you unscramble them?

ACEHPR   _____

TEACSNMRA   _____

GALNE   _____

MTLEPE   _____

HPTREPO   _____

RRAMYT   _____

SLOTUC   _____

WORD BANK

ANGEL
LOCUST
MARTYR
PREACH
PROPHET
SACRAMENT
TEMPLE

Answers on page 79

At a BAPTISM

You might find these people and things at a baptism today.

Priest — The priest leads the sacrament of baptism and welcomes us into the Christian community.

Sacred oils — The priest anoints us with sweet-smelling oil to remind us how much God loves us.

Baptismal font — This is filled with holy water. The water reminds us that baptism cleans away sin and gives us new life in Jesus.

Baptismal gown — At baptism we wear white clothing to symbolize our new life as a child of God.

Baptismal candle — The baptismal candle represents Jesus as the light of the world.

Family—Your parents try to live like Jesus did, and wanted you baptized so you will, too.

Godparents—These relatives or friends of your parents will support you in your faith.

SIMPLE SUDOKU

Can you complete the puzzle? Each row, column, and block
can contain only one instance of all the numbers 1 through 4.

Answer on page 79

SAINTS AND SACRAMENTS

Padre Pio

Holy Orders

Maximilian Kolbe

Matrimony

Louis and Zélie Martin

Reconciliation

John Vianney

Anointing of the Sick

Philip Neri

Baptism

Teresa of Ávila

Confirmation

John the Baptist

Eucharist

Draw a line from the saint to the correct sacrament.

Answer on page 80

FORGIVENESS QUIZ

When should you say "I'm sorry" and ask for forgiveness? Here are some clues to help you remember. Can you unscramble them?

1. Mom wouldn't buy candy in the checkout line, so I cried and had a EPRETM tantrum.

_____

2. My friend came to my house to play, but I would not EASRH my toys with her.

_____

3. When I wanted to go outside to play, Dad said I had to clean my room, so I sat on my bed and UPEDOT. _____

4. I threw a ball, and it broke our neighbor's window. When he asked if I knew what happened, I DILE and said I did not.

_____

5. I forgot to study for a test, so at school I TEADEHC and looked at another student's answers. _____

WORD BANK	CHEATED	POUTED	TEMPER
	LIED	SHARE	

Answers on page 80

NUMBER QUIZ

In the Bible, Jesus said we should be ready to forgive someone not just seven times, but seventy-seven times. That's a big number! Can you fill in the blank beneath each group of coins with the correct number?

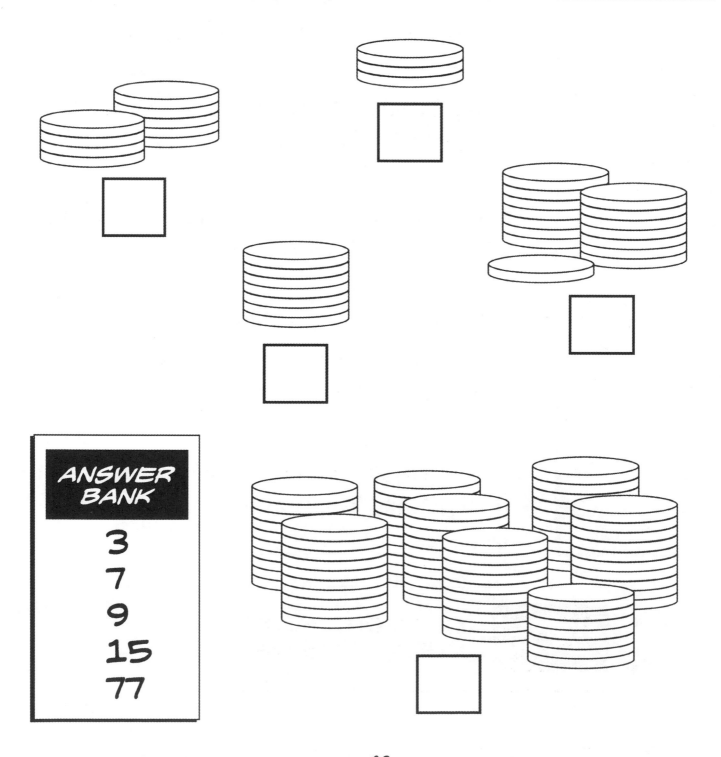

ANSWER BANK

3
7
9
15
77

ANIMALS OF
PADRE PIO'S NEIGHBORHOOD

dog

whale

cow

goose

lion

sheep

horse

pig

giraffe

Padre Pio grew up on a family farm in Italy. Can you circle 6 animals that he might find near his home?

Saint Padre Pio,
You helped many
people
through your
prayers and
advice.
Help me to
remember
to pray for
others—
especially those
who are sad or
hurting.
Amen.

ACT OF CONTRITION

This is a prayer that tells Jesus we are sorry for our sins. Complete the prayer by filling in the blanks with the missing words from the word bank.

Dear Jesus,

I am trying very hard to be

_____. I am

_____ for the times

I have _____ today.

_____ I will try

again. I know that you and the

_____ will help me

because you are so good.

I _____ you. _____.

 **WORD BANK**

AMEN
FAILED
SORRY

FATHER
GOOD

LOVE
TOMORROW

Answers on page 81

PADRE PIO CROSSWORD

Here is a crossword puzzle based on the Padre Pio book. In each clue there is a word in capital letters. Write this word in the correct spot in the puzzle.

ACROSS

1. Padre means FATHER in Italian.
3. Padre Pio's wounds of Jesus, the STIGMATA, were a special gift from God.
5. Young Brother Pio always had a ROSARY in his hand.
7. Pio's first name was FRANCESCO.
10. Padre Pio said, "You need to DUST a room every week."
11. Padre Pio is known as a saint for RECONCILIATION.

DOWN

2. Padre Pio's big dream was to build a HOSPITAL.
4. CONFESSION is another name for reconciliation.
6. When Padre Pio offered Mass, he prayed very SLOWLY.
8. Brother Pio studied to be a priest in a CAPUCHIN friary.
9. SIN hurts our friendship with God and others.

Answers on page 81

WORD JUMBLE

These words from the Padre Pio book are all mixed up!
Can you unscramble them?

TTASIAGM   _____

ERAGC   _____

ANIDROTNIO   _____

AMENSTRCAS   _____

HTRORBE   _____

SFREOONCS   _____

NCNEIOAZ   _____

WORD BANK

BROTHER
CANONIZE
CONFESSOR
GRACE
ORDINATION
SACRAMENTS
STIGMATA

Answers on page 82

23

A GIFT FROM JESUS

With the sacrament of reconciliation comes a very special gift from Jesus. Solve the rebus to see what that gift is.

Answer: _____

_____

Answers on page 82

WORD SEARCH

Find these 10 words from the Teresa of Ávila book! The words can be straight across, backward, up, down, or diagonal.

```
C N U N S H E S L T
I O N P C A U P M N
V R M R Y S C A I E
I H U M I D H I Z V
Z H K C U K A N I N
C P K Z V N R Z P O
L A U T I R I P S C
J O Y F U L S O N Q
T X C K U W T D N N
C A R M E L I T E S
```

WORD BANK

CARMELITE   JOYFUL
CHURCH   NUN
COMMUNION   SICK
CONVENT   SPAIN
EUCHARIST   SPIRITUAL

Answers on page 83

FOLLOW TERESA
THROUGH SPAIN!

Teresa traveled all over Spain to start new convents.
Connect the stars to these places in Spain.

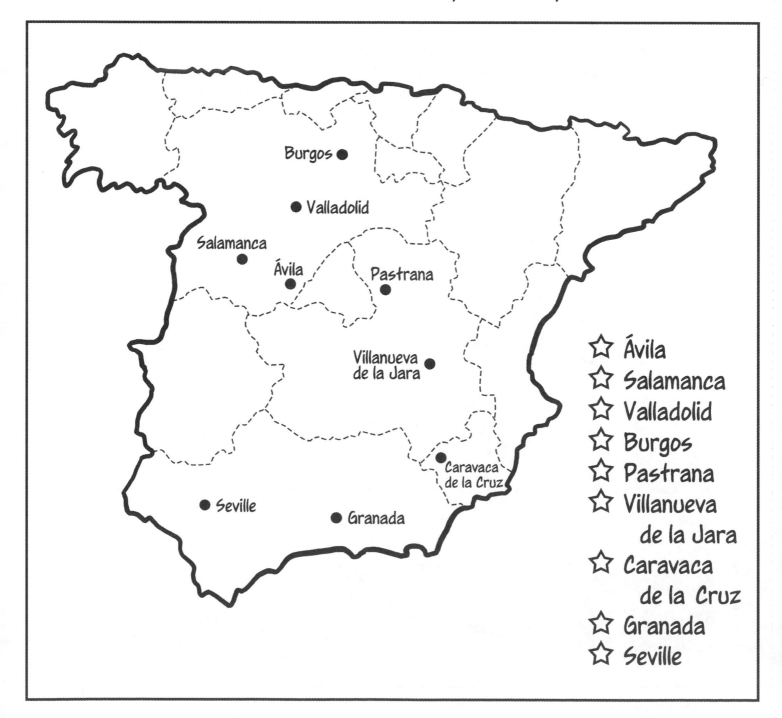

☆ Ávila
☆ Salamanca
☆ Valladolid
☆ Burgos
☆ Pastrana
☆ Villanueva
   de la Jara
☆ Caravaca
   de la Cruz
☆ Granada
☆ Seville

PRAYER TO TERESA OF ÁVILA

Saint Teresa of Ávila,
Help me to live a holy
and joyful life.
Like you,
may my heart
be open to Jesus.
Jesus is my friend.
He is all I need
to be happy.
Amen.

TERESA OF ÁVILA

CROSSWORD

Here is a crossword puzzle based on the Teresa of Ávila book. Write the missing word from the word bank in the correct spot in the puzzle.

ACROSS

5. Teresa is known as a saint for the _____ .
6. Another name for the Eucharist is _____ .
9. Teresa wrote, "Try to be _____ , like Jesus."
10. The Body and Blood of _____ is really present in the Eucharist.

DOWN

1. Teresa traveled around Spain to start new _____ convents.
2. Teresa was raised in a large family in _____ .
3. _____ brought Teresa peace.
4. Teresa learned to be a _____ at a convent.
7. Teresa prayed to _____ when she was sad or afraid.
8. Teresa wrote _____ about her life and work.

WORD BANK

BOOKS   JESUS
CARMELITE   MARY
COMMUNION   NUN
EUCHARIST   PRAYING
HOLY   SPAIN

Answers on page 83

30

SIMPLE SUDOKU

Can you complete the puzzle? Each row, column, and block can contain only one instance of all the numbers 1 through 4.

Answers on page 84

WORD JUMBLE

These words from the Teresa of Ávila book are all mixed up!
Can you unscramble them?

SAMS _____

AEGCR _____

ECTAIRLME _____

TESUICRHA _____

NVCNOTE _____

ALTRSIPUI _____

NMCMOIUON _____

WORD BANK

CARMELITE
CONVENT
EUCHARIST
GRACE
COMMUNION
MASS
SPIRITUAL

Answers on page 84

dot-to-dot

Connect the dots to complete the scene at the Carmelite convent.

MAZE

Help Teresa find her way through the walled city of Ávila, back to her convent.

Tic-Tac-Toe

seesaw

football

hopscotch

horseshoes

walking on
stilts

GAMES OF ITALY

Help Philip find his way through the walled city of Rome
to pray in the catacombs.

HIDDEN HELP

God the Father knows how really good you can be. If you need help to become the best YOU of all, there is Someone who can show you the way. Solve the rebus to see who your Helper is.

Answer: _____

_____

Answers on page 85

PRAYER TO PHILIP NERI

Saint Philip Neri,
The Holy Spirit filled you
with special gifts.
You were kind, happy,
and full of joy!
You led people
to Jesus.
Help me share
the joy of
my faith
with others.
Amen.

PHILIP NERI

CROSSWORD

Here is a crossword puzzle using words from the Philip Neri book. In each clue there is a word in capital letters. Write this word in the correct spot in the puzzle.

Answers on page 85

ACROSS

2. Some of the first Christians are buried in CATACOMBS.

4. Philip liked to spend time PRAYING.

5. Philip Neri is called the "saint of JOY."

6. Father Neri loved to celebrate MASS.

8. Philip often prayed to the HOLY SPIRIT.

10. Philip was born in FLORENCE, Italy.

DOWN

1. The Holy Spirit comes to us again at CONFIRMATION.

3. Father Neri led a group called the Congregation of the ORATORY.

7. Philip organized groups to help the POOR in Rome.

9. ROME was a large city with big problems.

COLOR THE EMOJIS

FIND THE HIDDEN OBJECTS

balloon

flag

pencil

eyeglasses

book

cup

cat

coin

Answers on page 86

WORD JUMBLE

These words from the Philip Neri book are all mixed up!
Can you unscramble them?

EEECENRVR   _____

ACFIORINNTOM   _____

NTOOIDAINR   _____

SACAMTSNER   _____

PTSBMIA   _____

SBOCMTAAC   _____

OEMR   _____

WORD BANK

BAPTISM
CATACOMBS
CONFIRMATION
ORDINATION
REVERENCE
ROME
SACRAMENTS

Answers on page 86

Fill the PICNIC BASKET

apple

picnic blanket

barbell

bottle opener

soda pop

saw

cake

sandwich

skunk

46

LOUIS + ZÉLIE MARTIN

FLOWERS OF FRANCE

iris

lily

sunflower

poppy

lavender

daffodil

multicolored
rose

Christmas
poinsettia

LOUIS AND ZÉLIE MARTIN

C R O S S W O R D

Here is a crossword puzzle based on the Louis and Zélie Martin book.
Write the missing word from the word bank in the correct spot in the puzzle.

WORD BANK

CANONIZED
CONVENT
FISH
FRANCE
GOD
LACE
MATRIMONY
THÉRÈSE
VISITATION
WATCH

ACROSS

2. Eventually all five Martin daughters joined a _____.
4. The Martins' youngest daughter, _____, is also a saint.
5. As a boy, Louis like to hike and _____.
7. The Martins are the first married couple to be _____ together.
9. _____ is another word for marriage.

DOWN

1. Louis worked as a _____ maker.
3. Leonie joined the _____ convent.
5. Both Zélie and Louis lived in _____.
6. Louis and Zélie Martin always put _____ first.
8. Zélie started her own _____-making business.

PRAYER TO
LOUIS AND
ZÉLIE MARTIN

Saints Louis and Zélie,
You loved God and you loved
each other very much.
Your children filled you
with joy and happiness.
You shared your faith
and your holiness.
Help my family to become
holy like yours.
Amen.

SPOT THE
DIFFERENCES
DIFFERENCES

These two pictures of Louis and Zélie aren't quite the same.
Can you find 6 differences?

Answers on page 87

Help Louis find his way through the forest to his wife, Zélie.

52

At a Wedding

prayer book

bouquet

cross

rings

candle

skateboard

veil

Which of these does NOT belong in a wedding?

WORD JUMBLE

These words from the Louis and Zélie Martin book are all mixed up!
Can you unscramble them?

ARKHMAWETC   _____

CNAONLE   _____

IACTOVNO   _____

IOSNTTIAVI   _____

ISIXULE   _____

LAMEETIRC   _____

RSNTAEMOY   _____

WORD BANK

ALENÇON
CARMELITE
LISIEUX
MONASTERY
VISITATION
VOCATION
WATCHMAKER

Answers on page 88

54

A Love Letter

Write a letter or poem to Jesus,
telling him how much you love him!

Tic-Tac-Toe

SUITING UP

Draw a line from the object to the place
it belongs on the soldier's body.

MAZE

Help John Vianney find his way to the lost sheep.

Prayer to
John Vianney

Saint John Vianney,
You loved God with
all your heart.
You brought many people to
him by your words
and actions.
Help me to be humble
and holy like you,
so I can help other people.
Amen.

WORD SEARCH

Find these 10 words from the John Vianney book! The words can be straight across, backward, up, down, or diagonal.

```
B  W  P  C  C  E  Y  W  E  N
W  I  B  A  L  Y  J  I  O  L
G  W  S  B  S  P  S  I  E  C
H  D  M  H  E  T  T  Z  C  I
Z  U  E  E  O  A  O  V  N  P
H  D  H  L  N  P  X  R  A  R
N  S  D  I  A  R  S  A  R  I
G  O  D  H  X  L  Q  D  F  E
G  R  D  R  E  H  P  E  H  S
O  P  A  R  I  S  H  C  E  T
```

WORD BANK

ARS	PARISH
BISHOP	PASTOR
FRANCE	PRIEST
HUMBLE	SHEEP
ORDINATION	SHEPHERD

Answers on page 88

Draw a line from the object or article of clothing to where it belongs on the priest.

WORD JUMBLE

These words from the John Vianney book are all mixed up!
Can you unscramble them?

ARLDLIYD _____

EMRSANYI _____

LIMHYO _____

OATSPR _____

OCOVITNA _____

OFNCOSLNIESA _____

RIOOIANDTN _____

WORD BANK

CONFESSIONAL
DARDILLY
HOMILY
ORDINATION
PASTOR
SEMINARY
VOCATION

Answers on page 89

WHO'S WHO AT YOUR PARISH?

The PASTOR is a priest who leads the parish. He celebrates the sacraments, preaches the gospel, and takes care of God's people.

The DEACON assists the priest, especially in celebrating the Mass.

The ALTAR SERVER is often an older boy or girl who serves at Mass and other liturgical functions and assists the priest at the altar.

The EUCHARISTIC MINISTER helps distribute Communion during Mass.

The MUSIC MINISTER coordinates the music at Mass and other worship events.

The USHER helps people find a place to worship and helps take the collection during Mass.

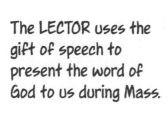

The LECTOR uses the gift of speech to present the word of God to us during Mass.

A RELIGIOUS SISTER may help out at church, and often works at a hospital, parish school, and so on.

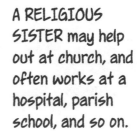

Tic-Tac-Toe

dot-to-dot

Connect the dots to complete the scene of John Vianney with his sheep.

WORD JUMBLE

These words from the Maximilian Kolbe book are all mixed up!
Can you unscramble them?

WORD BANK

CELL
GRACE
MARTYR
MISSIONARY
MONASTERY
ORDAINED
SACRAMENT

ACNSEATRM _____

CGERA _____

ISRMAOYSNI _____

LELC _____

ONRMESYAT _____

RDEONIDA _____

YTRMRA _____

Answers on page 89

PRAYER TO
MAXIMILIAN KOLBE

Saint Maximilian Kolbe,
you loved Jesus
and his mother, Mary.
Your heart was full of love
for other people.
Help me share my love
and think of others
before myself.
Amen.

dot-to-dot

Connect the dots to complete the scene of Maximilian Kolbe at the prison camp.

70

PRAYING THE Rosary

Second Mystery
Our Father
Begins 2nd Decade

Glory Be

Ten Hail Marys

Three
Hail Marys

Glory Be

End

First Mystery
Our Father
Begins 1st Decade

Our
Father

Ten Hail Marys

Apostles' Creed

Young Raymond Kolbe prayed the rosary every day to show his devotion to Mary, the Mother of God. This diagram shows how to pray the rosary.

SPOT THE
DIFFERENCES
DIFFERENCES

Can you circle 6 differences between the two pictures
of young Raymond Kolbe at home?

Answers on page 90

Maximilian Kolbe's
Sacrament

Father Maximilian did this to give peace and comfort to people. Starting at the arrow, read every other letter circling the picture to find out what it was.

Answer on page 90

Answer: _____

_____

 Jesus

 Healthy food

 A hug from Mom

 A puppy

Comfort and Healing

 A gift

 A teddy bear

 A doctor

Think about how these people or things can make you feel better when you are sick, worried, or sad.

SIMPLE SUDOKU

Can you complete the puzzle? Each row, column, and block can contain only one instance of all the numbers 1 through 4.

Answers on page 91

Tic-Tac-Toe

SAINTS FOR THE SACRAMENTS QUIZ

I lived in the desert and ate locusts and honey.

Padre Pio

I was a saint with stigmata.

Maximilian Kolbe

I began a Carmelite convent dedicated to prayer.

John Vianney

I grew up during the French Revolution.

Louis and Zélie Martin

We were the parents of Thérèse of Lisieux.

Philip Neri

I volunteered to die in place of a stranger in a prison camp.

Teresa of Ávila

My uncle wanted me to be a rich businessman.

John the Baptist

Draw a line from the clue to the correct saint.

Answers on page 91

JOHN'S STORY

Fill in the blanks in this short story about John the Baptist. Use the words from the word bank.

When John grew up, he went to the <u>DESERT</u> to pray and listen to God's voice. Then he traveled to the <u>JORDAN RIVER</u> to baptize and preach to his <u>DISCIPLES</u>. "Jesus the <u>MESSIAH</u> is coming soon! Get ready!" he said. When Jesus came, John <u>BAPTIZED</u> him. The <u>HOLY SPIRIT</u> came down as a <u>DOVE</u>. And a voice came from heaven, "You are my <u>SON</u>. I am pleased with you."

WORD BANK

BAPTIZED   HOLY SPIRIT
DESERT   JORDAN RIVER
DISCIPLES   MESSIAH
DOVE   SON

9

SPOT THE DIFFERENCES

Can you circle 6 differences between the two pictures of Jesus being baptized by John the Baptist?

8

78

WORD JUMBLE

These words from the John the Baptist book are all mixed up!
Can you unscramble them?

ACEHPR — PREACH

TEACSNMRA — SACRAMENT

GALNE — ANGEL

MTLEPE — TEMPLE

HPTREPO — PROPHET

RRAMYT — MARTYR

SLOTUC — LOCUST

12

WORD BANK

ANGEL
LOCUST
MARTYR
PREACH
PROPHET
SACRAMENT
TEMPLE

SIMPLE SUDOKU

Can you complete the puzzle? Each row, column, and block
can contain only one instance of all the numbers 1 through 4.

3	3	1	4	2
2	4	1	3
1	3	2	4
4	2	3	1

14

FORGIVENESS QUIZ

When should you say "I'm sorry" and ask for forgiveness? Here are some clues to help you remember. Can you unscramble them?

1. Mom wouldn't buy candy in the checkout line, so I cried and had a EPRETM tantrum.   TEMPER

2. My friend came to my house to play, but I would not EASRH my toys with her.   SHARE

3. When I wanted to go outside to play, Dad said I had to clean my room, so I sat on my bed and UPEDOT.   POUTED

4. I threw a ball, and it broke our neighbor's window. When he asked if I knew what happened, I DILE and said I did not.   LIED

5. I forgot to study for a test, so at school I TEADEHC and looked at another student's answers.   CHEATED

WORD BANK

CHEATED POUTED TEMPER
LIED SHARE

17

SAINTS AND SACRAMENTS

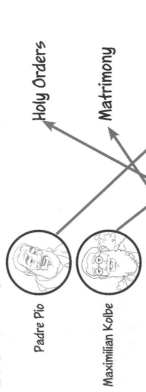

Padre Pio

Maximilian Kolbe

Louis and Zélie Martin

John Vianney

Philip Neri

Teresa of Ávila

John the Baptist

Holy Orders

Matrimony

Reconciliation

Anointing of the Sick

Baptism

Confirmation

Eucharist

Draw a line from the saint to the correct sacrament.

15

ACT OF CONTRITION

This is a prayer that tells Jesus we are sorry for our sins. Complete the prayer by filling in the blanks with the missing words from the word bank.

Dear Jesus,

I am trying very hard to be GOOD. I am

SORRY for the times today.

I have FAILED

TOMORROW I will try

again. I know that you and the

FATHER will help me

because you are so good.

I LOVE you. AMEN.

WORD BANK

AMEN	FATHER	LOVE
FAILED	GOOD	TOMORROW
SORRY		

PADRE PIO CROSSWORD

Here is a crossword puzzle based on the Padre Pio book. In each clue there is a word in capital letters. Write this word in the correct spot in the puzzle.

ACROSS

1. Padre means FATHER in Italian.
3. Padre Pio's wounds of Jesus, the STIGMATA, were a special gift from God.
5. Young Brother Pio always had a ROSARY in his hand.
7. Pio's first name was FRANCESCO.
10. Padre Pio said, "You need to DUST a room every week."
11. Padre Pio is known as a saint for RECONCILIATION.

DOWN

2. Padre Pio's big dream was to build a HOSPITAL.
4. CONFESSION is another name for reconciliation.
6. When Padre Pio offered Mass, he prayed very SLOWLY.
8. Brother Pio studied to be a priest in a CAPUCHIN friary.
9. SIN hurts our friendship with God and others.

A GIFT FROM JESUS

With the sacrament of reconciliation comes a very special gift from Jesus. Solve the rebus to see what that gift is.

C +  −

 + − L

+ − IF

Answer: C + PARROT − CARROT + LEAF − L + ICE − IF = PEACE

24

WORD JUMBLE

These words from the Padre Pio book are all mixed up! Can you unscramble them?

TTASIAGM	STIGMATA
ERAGC	GRACE
ANIDROTNIO	ORDINATION
AMENSTRCAS	SACRAMENTS
HTRORBE	BROTHER
SFREOONCS	CONFESSOR
NCNEIOAZ	CANONIZE

WORD BANK

BROTHER
CANONIZE
CONFESSOR
GRACE
ORDINATION
SACRAMENTS
STIGMATA

23

WORD SEARCH

Find these 10 words from the Teresa of Ávila book! The words can be straight across, backward, up, down, or diagonal.

```
C N U S H E S L T
I O N P C A U P M N
V R M R Y S C A I E
I H U M I D H I N V
Z H K C U K A N Z N
C P K Z V N R Z P O
L A U T I R I S R C
J O Y F U L S O N Q
T X C K U W T D N N
C A R M E L I T E S
```

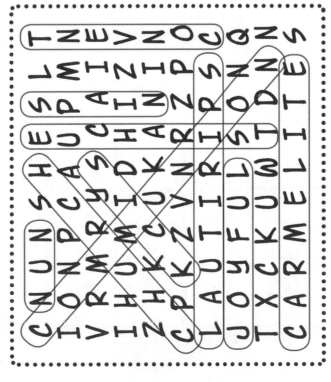

WORD BANK

CARMELITE
CHURCH
COMMUNION
CONVENT
EUCHARIST
JOYFUL
NUN
SICK
SPAIN
SPIRITUAL

27

TERESA OF ÁVILA
CROSSWORD

Here is a crossword puzzle based on the Teresa of Ávila book. Write the missing word from the word bank in the correct spot in the puzzle.

ACROSS

5. Teresa is known as a saint for the _____.
6. Another name for the Eucharist is _____.
9. Teresa wrote, "Try to be _____, like Jesus."
10. The Body and Blood of _____ is really present in the Eucharist.

DOWN

1. Teresa traveled around Spain to start new _____ convents.
2. Teresa was raised in a large family in _____.
3. _____ brought Teresa peace.
4. Teresa learned to be a _____ at a convent.
7. Teresa prayed to _____ when she was sad or afraid.
8. Teresa wrote _____ about her life and work.

WORD BANK

BOOKS
CARMELITE
COMMUNION
EUCHARIST
HOLY
JESUS
MARY
NUN
PRAYING
SPAIN

30

SIMPLE SUDOKU

Can you complete the puzzle? Each row, column, and block can contain only one instance of all the numbers 1 through 4.

3	1	2	4
2	4	1	3
1	3	4	2
4	2	3	1

32

WORD JUMBLE

These words from the Teresa of Ávila book are all mixed up! Can you unscramble them?

SAMS ___ MASS

AEGCR ___ GRACE

ECTAIRLME ___ CARMELITE

TESUICRHA ___ EUCHARIST

NVCNOTE ___ CONVENT

ALTRSIPUI ___ SPIRITUAL

NMCMOIUON ___ COMMUNION

WORD BANK
CARMELITE
CONVENT
EUCHARIST
GRACE
COMMUNION
MASS
SPIRITUAL

33

PHILIP NERI
CROSSWORD

Here is a crossword puzzle using words from the Philip Neri book. In each clue there is a word in capital letters. Write this word in the correct spot in the puzzle.

ACROSS

2. Some of the first Christians are buried in CATACOMBS.
4. Philip liked to spend time PRAYING.
5. Philip Neri is called the "saint of JOY."
6. Father Neri loved to celebrate MASS.
8. Philip often prayed to the HOLY SPIRIT.
10. Philip was born in FLORENCE, Italy.

DOWN

1. The Holy Spirit comes to us again at CONFIRMATION.
3. Father Neri led a group called the Congregation of the ORATORY.
7. Philip organized groups to help the POOR in Rome.
9. ROME was a large city with big problems.

42

HIDDEN HELP

God the Father knows how really good you can be. If you need help to become the best YOU of all, there is Someone who can show you the way. Solve the rebus to see who your Helper is.

Answer: $\underline{\text{JAR + M + M – ARM + NEST – N}}$
$\underline{+ \text{MOP – TOP – M + BUS – B = JESUS}}$

40

85

WORD JUMBLE

These words from the Philip Neri book are all mixed up!
Can you unscramble them?

EEECENRVR   REVERENCE

ACFIORINNTOM   CONFIRMATION

NTOOIDAINR   ORDINATION

SACAMTSNER   SACRAMENTS

PTSBMIA   BAPTISM

SBOCMTAAC   CATACOMBS

OEMR   ROME

WORD BANK

BAPTISM
CATACOMBS
CONFIRMATION
ORDINATION
REVERENCE
ROME
SACRAMENTS

45

FIND THE HIDDEN OBJECTS

balloon

pencil

book

cat

flag

eyeglasses

cup

coin

44

SPOT THE DIFFERENCES

These two pictures of Louis and Zélie aren't quite the same. Can you find 6 differences?

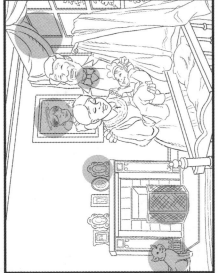

51

LOUIS AND ZÉLIE MARTIN
CROSSWORD

Here is a crossword puzzle based on the Louis and Zélie Martin book. Write the missing word from the word bank in the correct spot in the puzzle.

WORD BANK

CANONIZED
CONVENT
FISH
FRANCE
GOD
LACE
MATRIMONY
THÉRÈSE
VISITATION
WATCH

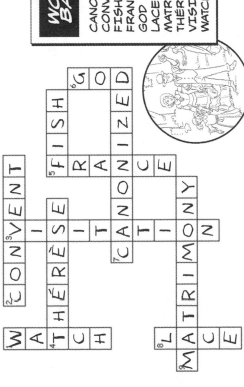

ACROSS
2. Eventually all five Martin daughters joined a _____.
4. The Martins' youngest daughter, _____, is also a saint.
5. As a boy, Louis like to hike and _____.
7. The Martins are the first married couple to be _____ together.
9. _____ is another word for marriage.

DOWN
1. Louis worked as a _____ maker.
3. Leonie joined the _____ convent.
5. Both Zélie and Louis lived in _____.
6. Louis and Zélie Martin always put _____ first.
8. Zélie started her own _____ -making business.

Crossword solution:
W
A   ²C O N V E N T
⁴T H É R È S E   ⁵F I S H
C   I   R   ⁶G
H   T   A   O
            ⁷C A N O N I Z E D
            T   C
            I   E
⁸L A T R I M O N Y
A
C
E

49

WORD SEARCH

Find these 10 words from the John Vianney book! The words can be straight across, backward, up, down, or diagonal.

WORD BANK

ARS
BISHOP
FRANCE
HUMBLE
ORDINATION

PARISH
PASTOR
PRIEST
SHEEP
SHEPHERD

61

WORD JUMBLE

These words from the Louis and Zélie Martin book are all mixed up! Can you unscramble them?

ARKHMAWETC — WATCHMAKER
CNAONLE — ALENÇON
IACTOVNO — VOCATION
IOSNTTIAVI — VISITATION
ISIXULE — LISIEUX
LAMEETIRC — CARMELITE
RSNTAEMOY — MONASTERY

WORD BANK

ALENÇON
CARMELITE
LISIEUX
MONASTERY
VISITATION
VOCATION
WATCHMAKER

54

WORD JUMBLE

These words from the Maximilian Kolbe book are all mixed up!
Can you unscramble them?

WORD BANK
CELL
GRACE
MARTYR
MISSIONARY
MONASTERY
ORDAINED
SACRAMENT

ACNSEATRM	SACRAMENT
CGERA	GRACE
ISRMAOYSNI	MISSIONARY
LELC	CELL
ONRMESYAT	MONASTERY
RDEONIDA	ORDAINED
YTRMRA	MARTYR

68

WORD JUMBLE

These words from the John Vianney book are all mixed up!
Can you unscramble them?

ARLDLIYD	DARDILLY
EMRSANYI	SEMINARY
LIMHYO	HOMILY
OATSPR	PASTOR
OCOVITNA	VOCATION
OFNCOSLNIESA	CONFESSIONAL
RIOOIANDTN	ORDINATION

WORD BANK
CONFESSIONAL
DARDILLY
HOMILY
ORDINATION
PASTOR
SEMINARY
VOCATION

63

Maximilian Kolbe's Sacrament

Father Maximilian did this to give peace and comfort to people. Starting at the arrow, read every other letter circling the picture to find out what it was.

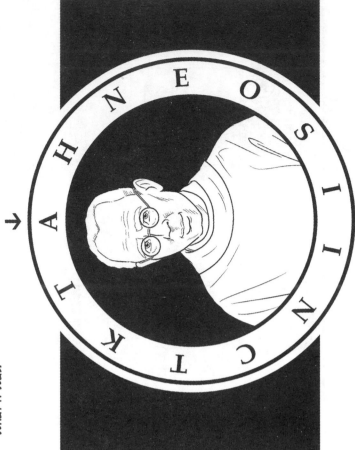

Answer: ANOINT THE SICK

73

SPOT THE DIFFERENCES

Can you circle 6 differences between the two pictures of young Raymond Kolbe at home?

72

SAINTS FOR THE SACRAMENTS QUIZ

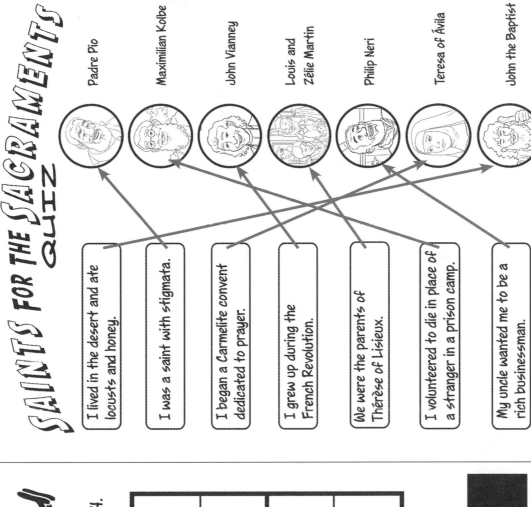

Padre Pio

Maximilian Kolbe

John Vianney

Louis and Zélie Martin

Philip Neri

Teresa of Ávila

John the Baptist

I lived in the desert and ate locusts and honey.

I was a saint with stigmata.

I began a Carmelite convent dedicated to prayer.

I grew up during the French Revolution.

We were the parents of Thérèse of Lisieux.

I volunteered to die in place of a stranger in a prison camp.

My uncle wanted me to be a rich businessman.

Draw a line from the clue to the correct saint.

77

SIMPLE SUDOKU

Can you complete the puzzle? Each row, column, and block can contain only one instance of all the numbers 1 through 4.

4	1	2	3
2	3	4	1
3	4	1	2
1	2	3	4

75

saint for sacraments

John the Baptist

Saint for Baptism

First century

Born in the hill country of Judea

Feast Days: June 24 (Birth)
August 29 (Martyrdom)

Patron saint of the Sacrament of Baptism, converts, and the country Jordan

Teresa of Ávila

Saint for the Eucharist

(also known as Teresa of Jesus)

1515-1582

Born in Ávila, Spain

Feast Day: October 15

Patron saint of people with headaches and Spanish Catholic writers

Padre Pio

Saint for Reconciliation

1887-1968

Born in Pietrelcina, Italy

Feast Day: September 23

Patron saint of confessors, stress relief, and the town of Pietrelcina

philip neri

louis + zélie martin

john vianney

maximilian kolbe

LOUIS and ZÉLIE MARTIN

Saints for Matrimony

Louis Martin
  1823-1894

Born in Bordeaux, France

Marie-Azélie "Zélie" Guérin Martin
  1831-1877

Born in Gandelain, France

Feast Day: July 12

PHILIP NERI

Saint for Confirmation

1515-1595

Born in Florence, Italy

Feast Day: May 26

Patron saint of Rome, joy, and
  US Army Special Forces

MAXIMILIAN KOLBE

Saint for Anointing of the Sick

1894-1941

Born in Zdunska Wola, Poland

Feast Day: August 14

Patron saint of the 20th century,
  journalists, prisoners, people with
  drug problems, families, and the
  prolife movement

JOHN VIANNEY

Saint for Holy Orders

(Also known as the Curé of Ars)

1786-1859

Born in Dardilly, France

Feast Day: August 4

Patron saint of parish priests and
  confessors